KEITH PIRT COLOUR PORTFOLIO

Irish Railways in Colour – Volume 1

Keith R. Pirt

Compiled by Roger Hill and Hugh Ballantyne

BOOK LAW PUBLICATIONS

Copyright Book Law Publications 2010

ISBN 978-1-907094-97-2

INTRODUCTION

The Publishers, having agreed with Keith Pirt before his untimely death in 2005 to publish Keith's work in landscape format, are now pleased to offer this selection of his historic colour photographs taken in Ireland.

In this volume you will find pictures taken during three visits. The first took place in July 1956 at a time when the Cavan and Leitrim three-foot gauge line was still open and there was a huge variety of locomotives to be seen on the five-foot three-inch gauge, many of which had rapidly disappeared before Keith's second visit in July/August 1959. This was just in time for him to obtain some splendid images of the three-foot gauge County Donegal Railway before it closed at the end of that year. The third trip, in June 1961, seems to have coincided with a railtour which travelled to the west of Ireland, but after the last of all the Irish narrow gauge lines, the West Clare, had closed five months earlier. In all three cases Keith was extraordinarily lucky with the weather, most of his Irish pictures were taken in good sunlight, little of the infamous "soft" Irish days were evident!

As a brief historical reminder, during the time span of these visits there were four Irish five-foot three-inch gauge and three three-foot narrow gauge railways in operation. In the Republic there was Coras Iompair Eireann, formed in 1945 on nationalisation of the Great Southern Railways. This latter Railway was created in 1925 from three main railways, plus some lesser ones which, for just one year in 1924, called themselves the Great Southern Railway. Today the railway in the Republic is known as Irish Rail.

The two five-foot three-inch cross-border railways were, first the Great Northern Railway Ireland, which became bankrupt in 1953 and then operated as the Great Northern Railway Board until 1958, when the locomotive stock was divided equally between the two managing railways, CIE and the Ulster Transport Authority. Secondly, there was the Sligo Leitrim and Northern Counties Railway, which operated between Enniskillen and Sligo until it closed in 1957.

Self contained within Northern Ireland was the Ulster Transport Authority which was formed in 1948 by the vesting of the Northern Ireland Road Transport Board and the Belfast & County Down Railway. The NCC which was owned by the LMS, was subject to nationalisation on the first day of January 1948, and thereby required its railway interests in Northern Ireland to be divested. The NCC became nationalised into the UTA in 1949 and, in 1968, the very much reduced railway network in the Province became Northern Ireland Railways.

Lastly, the County Donegal Railways Joint Committee operated the cross-border three-foot gauge County Donegal Railway under the jurisdiction of the GNR and the NCC, and their successors, until it closed on 31 December 1959.

Finally, we should like to thank Lance King and John K Williams for the information and assistance which they have so kindly given.

ABBREVIATIONS

C & L	Cavan & Leitrim Railway	IRRS	Irish Railway Record Society
CB & PR	Cork Blackrock & Passage Railway	LMS	London Midland & Scottish Railway
CDR	County Donegal Railway	MGWR	Midland Great Western Railway
CDRJC	County Donegal Railways Joint Committee	NCC	Northern Counties Committee
CIE	Coras Iompair Eireann	NIR	Northern Ireland Railways
DSER	Dublin & South Eastern Railway	RPSI	Railway Preservation Society of Ireland
GNR	Great Northern Railway Ireland	SECR	South Eastern & Chatham Railway
GNRB	Great Northern Railway Ireland Board	SL & NCR	Sligo Leitrim and Northern Counties Railway
GSR	Great Southern Railways	UTA	Ulster Transport Authority
GSWR	Great Southern & Western Railway		

Front cover picture: Following upgrading of the GNR main line between Belfast and Dublin, and rebuilding of the River Boyne Viaduct at Drogheda, in 1932, the axle load was permitted to be raised to twenty one tons. The Company ordered five three-cylinder compound locomotives from Beyer Peacock, which were delivered in the same year. Immaculate in its impressive blue livery, Class V 4-4-0 85 MERLIN is standing ex-works on Dundalk shed in July 1956. Fortunately MERLIN is preserved and in 2010 is undergoing overhaul for a return to service.

BLP - C28

First published in the United Kingdom by Book Law Publications 2010 — 382 Carlton Hill, Nottingham, NG4 1JA

Printed and bound by The Amadeus Press, Cleckheaton, West Yorkshire

A scene at Belturbet, the terminus of the GNR four and a quarter miles long branch from Ballyhaise. Here the GNR met with the northern end of the three-foot gauge C & L line of CIE, with the narrow gauge running into a bay platform at the other side of the covered station. The engine is Class JT 2-4-2T 91, built at Dundalk in 1902 to the design of Charles Clifford. 91 is on its regular job, waiting to depart for Ballyhaise, which enabled passengers to connect with trains for Clones and beyond.   (July 1956). *BLP - C14*

At Amiens Street, the GNR's main station in Dublin (now known as Connolly). is Class S 4-4-0 170 ERRIGAL, seen shunting CIE liveried coaching stock on the northern side of the station where the connecting line of CIE came across the City from Westland Row (now Pearse) station. 170 was built by Beyer Peacock in 1913 and taken into CIE stock when the assets of the GNRB were divided between the UTA and CIE in December 1958. This locomotive was named after the highest mountain in County Donegal. (July 1961). *BLP - C17*

An attractive portrait of Class U 4-4-0 198 LOUGH SWILLY standing at Dundalk waiting to take the Bundoran Express, arriving from Dublin, on the remainder of its journey across the north west of Ireland to the coastal resort of Bundoran, a distance of 105 miles from Dundalk. 198 was one of five locomotives built by Beyer Peacock in 1915 (followed by another five in 1948). It was taken into CIE stock in 1958 and then sold on to the UTA in 1963, where it remained in service for a further two years. (July 1956). *BLP - C13*

A fine picture of Class W 2-6-0 91 THE BUSH, built at Derby in 1933, one of fifteen mixed traffic locomotives built for the NCC and popularly known as "Moguls". Four were built at Derby and eleven assembled at York Road Works, Belfast, from sets of parts sent over from Derby. The engine is seen on the turntable at Dundalk, nice and clean in the UTA livery of black, lined red and yellow. Twelve of the class were named, this being one of five bearing names of Rivers in Northern Ireland. 91 was withdrawn in 1965.   (July 1961). *BLP - C16*

Well cleaned in its plain black livery is CIE Class J15b 0-6-0 719, seen at Amiens Street, Dublin. This locomotive was one of a class of ten built by the GSR at Inchicore Works in Dublin, in 1935 and withdrawn in 1962.
(July 1961). *BLP - C19*

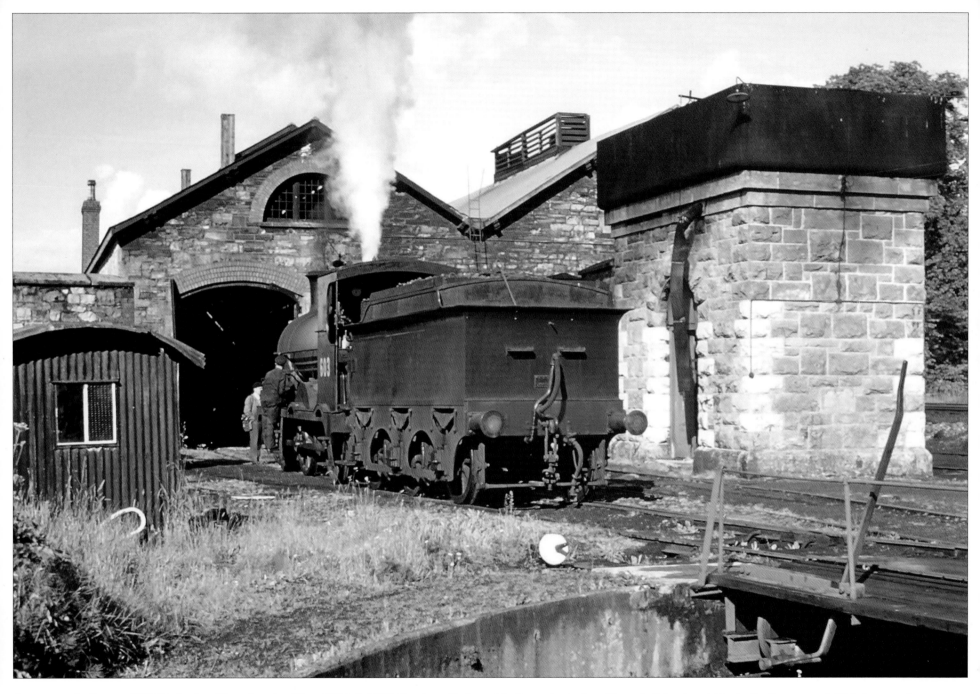

A scene at the former MGWR shed at Sligo showing Class J19 0-6-0 603 blowing off alongside the water tank, with part of the turntable in the foreground. This locomotive was one of a class of twenty, built by the MGWR in 1888 at its Broadstone Works in Dublin.

(July 1961). *BLP - C20*

A portrait outside Sligo shed of a classic Victorian era product from Beyer Peacock's Gorton Foundry. This is HAZLEWOOD, one of five "Leitrim" Class 0-6-4Ts supplied to the SL & NCR, three in 1882 and this one, the last of two in 1899. These locomotives displayed many standard Beyer Peacock features of the time, having a low parallel boiler, large bell mouthed steam dome and two square windows in the cab front sheet. The SL & NCR was unique in that all its locomotives carried only names, no numbers, HAZLEWOOD being the name of a residence of one of the directors of the Railway. This engine remained in service until the Railway closed on 1 October 1957. Sadly an attempt to preserve it in the Belfast Transport Museum was unsuccessful and it fell into the hands of the scrap man in 1959.

(July 1956). *BLP - C1059*

Sparkling in the sunshine at Amiens Street is Class S 4-4-0 174 CARRANTUOHILL, showing off to perfection the blue livery in which the GNR painted selected passenger engine classes. The blue has been described as "azure" blue, lined black and white. The footplate edging is vermilion edged white, the buffer beam vermilion edged black and the nameplate brass, with sunken letters painted black. It was named after the highest mountain in Ireland, 3,414 feet above sea level in County Kerry. Sister engine 171 SLIEVE GULLION is one of Ireland's most outstanding, reliable and popular preserved locomotives.

(July 1961). *BLP - C15*

Cleaned and coaled in readiness for railtour duty, Class J18 0-6-0 588 stands outside Athlone shed. This engine was built for the MGWR by Sharp Stewart in 1885 and withdrawn by CIE in 1963. *(July 1961). BLP - C18*

A well worn survivor was MGWR Class G2 2-4-0 655, easing on to the turntable outside the small shed at Ballaghaderreen, situated at the terminus of a branch line from Kilfree Junction , on the main line to Sligo, in County Roscommon.. This locomotive was one of twenty built by the MGWR in 1897 and, when photographed in June 1961, had already outlived the last 2-4-0 type in Great Britain by three years.

BLP - C21

Regarded by some as the most attractive locomotives of the former DSER were two 2-6-0s designed by George Wild, and built by Beyer Peacock in 1922. The pair were an enlargement of a goods engine type dating from 1904 but incorporating a pony truck. They spent most of their lives working the Wexford goods, but here 461 (which is now preserved) is at Dungarvan hauling an enthusiasts special in June 1961.

BLP - C24

13

The pride of the GSR fleet were the three Class B1a three-cylinder 4-6-0s designed by E C Bredin and built at Inchicore in 1939. Their introduction permitted an acceleration of the Dublin to Cork mail trains, but following rapid dieselisation of CIE in the early 1950s their full potential was never realised. The three engines were named after Irish Queens and here 800 MAEDHBH (a Queen of Connaught) is seen in the shed yard at Thurles, by then earmarked for preservation. It is now preserved in the Ulster Folk & Transport Museum at Cultra, painted in the attractive green livery of the GSR.
(July 1961). *BLP - C25*

A portrait of CIE Class I3 0-6-2T 673 outside Amiens Street shed, one of five engines built at Inchicore in 1933 and used on the Dublin and South Eastern section suburban services. (July 1961). *BLP - C26*

Standing at the narrow gauge platform at Belturbet station is former CB & PR 2-4-2T 10L ready to leave with its train to Ballinamore, awaiting the arrival of the GNR broad gauge branch train from Ballyhaise. (July 1956). *BLP - C31*

Ballinamore shed yard on the C & L three-foot gauge section, seen to good effect in summer evening sunlight. On the left is 10L, one of the four ex CB & PR 2-4-2Ts which were transferred to the C & L in 1934 after their home Railway had closed in 1932. These engines were built by Neilson in 1900 and had, at four-foot six-inches diameter, the largest driving wheels and maximum axle load, at eleven tons eleven hundredweight, of any Irish narrow gauge locomotives. On the right is 8L, one of the eight original C & L 4-4-0Ts dating from 1887. After the railway was closed on 31 March 1959, 10L was used to haul demolition trains on the Belturbet line and was cut up when that work was completed. (July 1956). *BLP - C33*

17

A lovely portrait of a GSWR 4-4-0 passenger engine designed by a well known Locomotive Engineer from Inchicore Works, J A F Aspinall. It was built in 1885 and became Class D14 85. It is seen in July 1956 being prepared for work outside Inchicore shed and saw another three years service before withdrawal.

BLP - C34

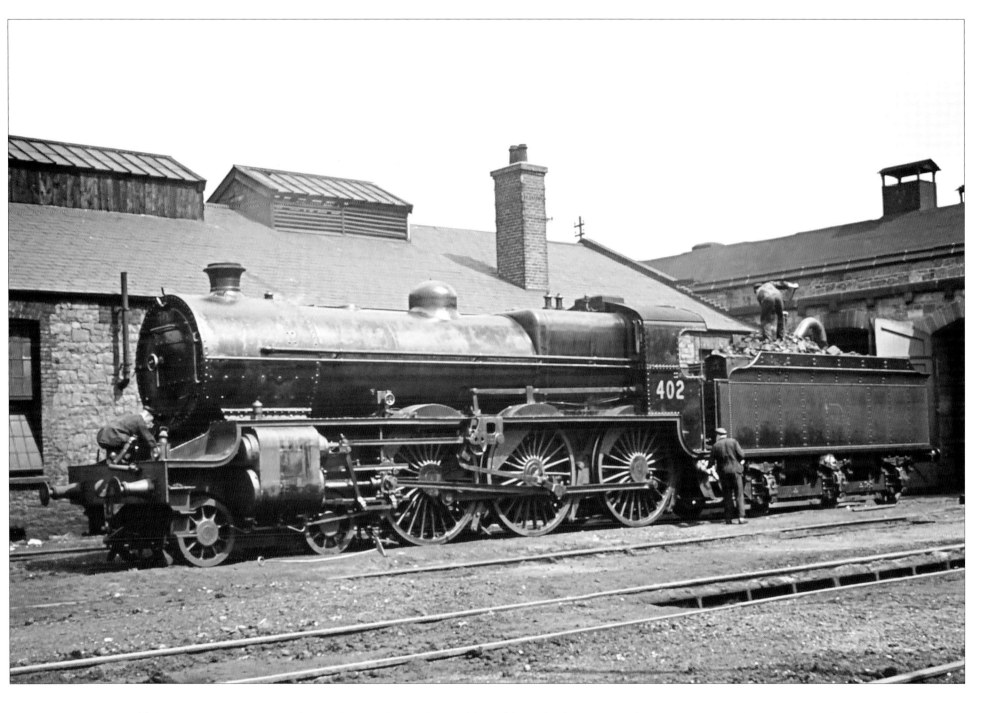

A former GSWR 4-6-0 which became Class B2a 402, being made ready for service outside Inchicore shed. It was one of ten locomotives designed by Edward Watson as a superheated four-cylinder type, the first appearing during 1916 and the following nine after the First World War. 402 was built at Inchicore in 1921 and rebuilt in 1927 with two cylinders. Two more were built at Inchicore in 1921 and the remaining six by Armstrong Whitworth a year later. (July 1956). *BLP - C383*

Shunting coaching stock at Sligo station on the former MGWR system is Class J19 0-6-0 610 which was built at Broadstone Works in 1888 and withdrawn by CIE aged 75 in 1963. (July 1956). *BLP - C36*

GNR Class AL 0-6-0 56 is shunting in Clones yard. Clones was on the old Irish North Western Railway main line and a junction for lines to Portadown and Cavan. 56 was built at Dundalk in 1895 and passed to the UTA in 1958 when the assets of the GNRB were divided. It was withdrawn in 1960.
(July 1956). *BLP - C37*

A classic Irish railcar seen on the GNR at Clones, apparently shunting backwards and propelling its small trailer towards the station. This was Railcar C1, built at Dundalk in 1934. Its engine and driving section were articulated from the main body. It had a Gardner 96 hp diesel engine and four-speed gearbox, but could only be driven from the front end. One class accommodation was provided for 56 passengers. It mainly worked the Enniskillen to Bundoran line and was stated to be running nearly a thousand miles per week on 12 mpg of diesel.

(July 1956). *BLP - C38*

Clearly a bus on rails! This is Railbus 8177 (were there really another 8,176 of them?!!), which was converted from a road bus in July 1935 for the Dundalk, Newry & Greenore Railway. It was bought by the GNR in 1948 and transferred to the Civil Engineers stock who renumbered it 8177 in 1956. It is seen here on the turntable at Dundalk. In 1958 it passed into CIE stock and its eventual fate is unknown to your compilers. Would any reader who knows please be kind enough to contact the Publishers? (July 1956). *BLP - C39*

On the cross-border SL & NCR, Manorhamilton was, both in the operating and geographical senses, the centre of the Railway and the location of its Locomotive and Carriage & Wagon Works. This is a view looking towards Enniskillen of "Lough" Class 0-6-4T LOUGH ERNE waiting to continue its journey from Enniskillen to Sligo with a goods train. This locomotive was one of two built by Beyer Peacock in 1949 and the subject of a hire purchase agreement between the makers and the SL & NCR. The Railway closed in 1957 and in 1959 the two engines were sold by Beyer Peacock to the UTA. LOUGH ERNE became UTA 27 and retained its name until withdrawn by NIR in 1970. It is now preserved at the RPSI site at Whitehead, County Antrim.

(July 1956). *BLP - C42*

A splendid picture of two of the GNR's finest at Great Victoria Street Station, Belfast in July 1956. On the left is Class VS 4-4-0 210 ERNE ready to depart south with a Dublin express and alongside is Class V compound 4-4-0 86 PEREGRINE. These two classes, comprising five in each, represented the high water mark of GNR express passenger locomotive types. Both were built by Beyer Peacock, 86 in 1932 and 210 in 1948. It is believed that the VS was the last 4-4-0 type ever to be built for a main line company. Both engines went to the UTA in 1958 and were withdrawn in 1963 and 1961 respectively.

BLP - C44

In ex-works condition, GNR Class RT 0-6-4T 22 is seen shunting in Grosvenor Street Goods Yard, Belfast, its 1908 Beyer Peacock makers plate prominent on the sandbox. This was another locomotive which passed to the UTA in 1958 and was soon withdrawn.

(July 1956). *BLP - C46*

Another fine Victorian era built GSWR locomotive seen still at work at over 70 years of age. CIE Class D17 4-4-0 54 comes slowly past Inchicore shed with a southbound goods train from Dublin. This engine was built here in 1883 and withdrawn in 1959. *(July 1956). BLP - C48*

Standing outside Inchicore shed with its plain black livery well cleaned is Class D2 4-4-0 329. This attractive engine was originally built in 1906 to the design of Robert Coey at a time when the GSWR needed main line motive power. It was one of a class of twelve and was rebuilt as seen here in 1921. It was withdrawn in 1960.   (July 1956). *BLP - C49*

Another work weary locomotive on the narrow gauge C & L section is ex Tralee & Dingle 2-6-2T 5T, seen standing at Ballinamore with the daily through mixed train from Belturbet to Dromod. 5T was built by Hunslet in 1892 and was the third of four locomotives sent up (over a period of sixteen years!) to the C & L from Tralee. In their new home they were not surprisingly known to the staff as "The Kerrymen". 5T came to Ballinamore in 1949 and was worked hard until the Railway closed on 31 March 1959. Fortunately 5T has survived into preservation and is now back on its native heath on the Tralee & Dingle Preservation Railway at Blennerville, County Kerry. *(July 1956). BLP - C50*

Another classic Irish railbus, this being GNR No 1, seen at Dundalk. Not surprisingly it was converted from a road bus in September 1934 and was identified by the letter E. In 1947 it was renumbered 1 and was transferred to the Civil Engineer's stock shortly after Keith took this picture, where it was again renumbered, becoming 8178. In 1958 it passed to CIE and worked until 1963. It had a Gardner 4LW diesel engine of 60 hp and could seat 30 passengers. It is now preserved in the Ulster Folk & Transport Museum at Cultra.

(July 1956). *BLP - C55*

To combat ever increasing road competition in the 1920s/30s the GNR was a pioneer in the British Isles in implementing railcar and railbus services on secondary and branch lines. Whilst the railbuses were converted from existing road vehicles the railcars were custom built for rail use. Looking very stylish, considering it was built in 1936, is Railcar D, photographed in the yard at Dundalk. It consisted of two lightweight coach bodies, articulated to a central power bogie having three axles to which the coupled driving wheels were attached, and seated a total of 159 people. The engine was a Gardner 153 hp diesel with a four speed gearbox.
(July 1956). *BLP - C56*

In 1947 the SL & NCR took delivery of diesel Railcar B from Walker Brothers of Wigan. It was a bi-directional railcar consisting of a power unit and driving cab mounted on a four wheel bogie with outside connecting rods and an articulated passenger section seating 59 people, carried on another four wheel bogie. At the rear end were driving controls in a half cab let into the passenger section. As can be seen, it was a very smart vehicle, with manually operated sliding doors on each side and in the side windows were louvred ventilators. Its quoted fuel consumption was 12 mpg, giving very favourable operating costs of 4d (2p) per mile as against 2/6d (12 and a half pence) for a steam hauled train. After closure of the Railway in 1957 it was purchased by CIE for further use.

(July 1956). *BLP - C59*

This picture at Strabane shows to good effect the contrast between the five-foot three-inch and three-foot gauges of the GNR and the CDR. On the left is red liveried Class 5 2-6-4T 4 MEENGLAS, built by Nasmyth Wilson of Manchester in 1907 and to the right, GNR Class U 4-4-0 65 LOUGH MELVIN on a goods train. This locomotive was built by Beyer Peacock in 1915 as GNR 200, passed to the UTA in 1958 and was withdrawn in 1961. MEENGLAS was withdrawn when the CDR closed in December 1959 and is now preserved on the Foyle Valley Railway at Londonderry.

(August 1959). *BLP - C69*

Leaving the GNR terminus of Great Victoria Street, Belfast, is Class UG 0-6-0 47 with a train of stock comprising UTA green and GNR mahogany liveries. This engine was built at Dundalk in October 1937 as GNR 82 but is now seen here with its UTA number and attached to one of the post war tenders in the style of the Stanier designed LMS tenders.   (August 1959). *BLP - C74*

On an overcast day Class WT 2-6-4T 52 is passing Adelaide in the suburbs of Belfast with a long goods train. These engines were a post World War 2 design for the NCC supplied from Derby as a tank engine version of the pre war Class W 2-6-0s and bore a resemblance to the Stanier and Fairburn 2-6-4Ts of the LMS. The first four arrived in 1946 and thereafter another fourteen were built up to 1950, by which time the NCC had become part of the nationalised UTA.. No.52 was built in 1949 and withdrawn in 1968. The class was popularly known as "Jeeps", a reference to the war time US Army "General Purpose - Go Anywhere", four wheel drive car, the NCC staff having similar regard for the versatility and usefulness of the WTs. Three of the class continued in service on NIR until 1971 and so became the last steam locomotives in commercial use in the British Isles. No. 4 is now preserved and sees frequent charter train use.

(August 1959). *BLP - C75*

The GNR had this one crane tank, 0-6-0CT 31, seen at its home in the yard at Dundalk Works, where it was employed as Works shunter. It was built in 1928 by Hawthorn, Leslie and when the assets of the GNRB were divided between CIE and the UTA in 1958 this locomotive was the one exception. Dundalk Works was formed into a separate independent company, Dundalk Engineering Limited, and took ownership of 31. In 1960 however, the Company sold it to CIE which placed it into service stock until withdrawal in 1963. **(July 1956).** *BLP - C79*

36

This locomotive was built in 1875 as an 0-6-4T "carriage engine" by the GSWR at Inchicore for the Castleisland Railway, a four and a half mile long light railway south of Tralee. It was taken into GSWR stock in 1879 and in 1915 the carriage section was removed and the engine rebuilt into a conventional 0-6-0T. It continued in service, eventually becoming CIE Class J30 90 and was photographed by Keith at Cork in June 1961. It bears more than a passing resemblance to the English Brighton "Terriers". It is now preserved at Downpatrick in County Down and in 2007 became operational again.

BLP - C81

One of the many and versatile GSWR 0-6-0s, by now CIE Class J15. 125 is seen at Ballybrophy on the main line between Dublin and Limerick Junction, whilst working an IRRS charter train. No fewer than 111 J15s were built between 1866 and 1903, this example coming from Inchicore in 1881. It was rebuilt with a superheated Belpaire boiler in 1949 and remained in stock until 1965. Two J15s, 184 and 186, are preserved. *(June 1961). BLP - C82*

Henry Forbes, the Secretary and Traffic Manager of the CDRJC, foresaw the introduction of railcars as the means by which the CDR could counteract road competition and provide lower operating costs for their passenger services. They could also meet local needs such as the ability to stop anywhere to pick up or set down in the sparsely populated country served by the Railway. This is railcar 18 which was built by the GNR and Walker Brothers in 1940. It had a Gardner 6LW diesel engine of 102 hp and carried 43 passengers. It accidentally caught fire in 1949 and was rebuilt at Dundalk in 1950. This picture shows it shunting goods wagons in the yard at Stranorlar four months before closure of the Railway.   (August 1959). *BLP - C85*

A splendid sight on the three-foot gauge CDR showing 4 MEENGLAS, immaculate in red livery lined yellow, doing a spot of shunting at Castlefinn. The train was en route from Strabane to Stranorlar and this was the first station, six miles along the valley of the River Finn.

(August 1959). *BLP - C86*

By the time Keith went on an IRRS railtour to Ennis in June 1961, the West Clare three-foot gauge section of CIE had closed on the previous 31 January. In the yard however there were still interesting things to see and photograph before all was swept into oblivion. This was one of the three Bo-Bo diesel mechanicals which CIE had bought for the Railway in 1955. It is F503, built by Walker Brothers of Wigan, and was retained to shunt materials brought up the line by demolition trains. It had two Gardner 107 bhp 6LW engines, one each side of its centre cab, and could haul 170 tons on the level at 25 mph or 130 tons at 30 mph. After closure of the Railway the three locomotives were sent to Inchicore Works and, being comparatively new, were offered for sale, but as there were no takers they were scrapped in 1968/69.

BLP - C87

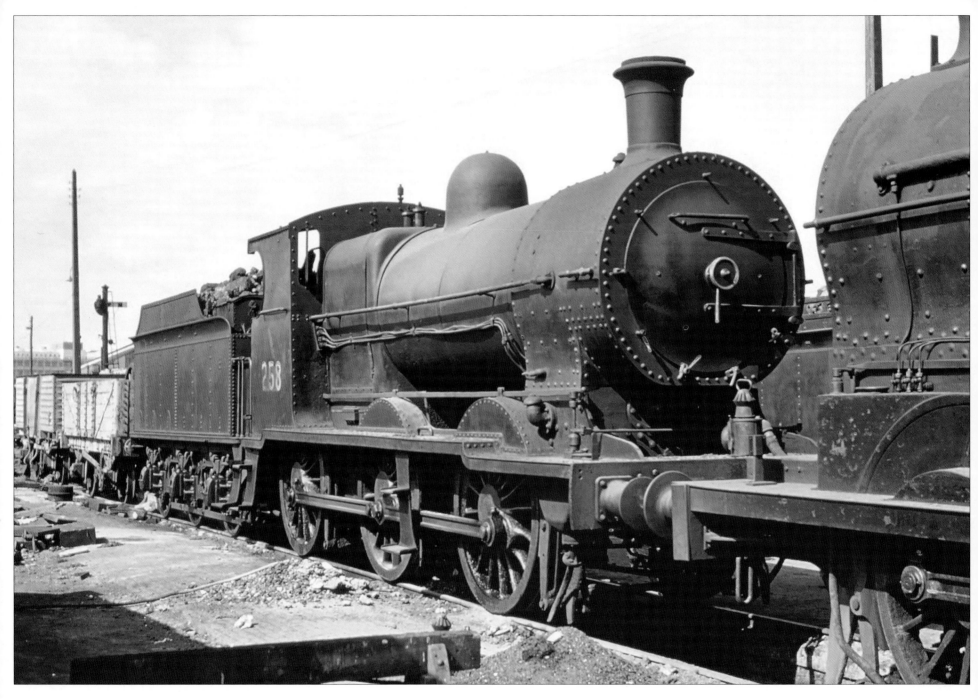

Standing outside Amiens Street shed in Dublin is CIE Class J4 0-6-0 258. It was one of eight goods engines designed by Robert Coey for the GSWR but not built until 1913, after he had retired. These engines were superheated and gave reliable service, 258 having a working life of 50 years.　　　　(June 1961). *BLP - C89*

Ex GNR Class Q 4-4-0 132 is waiting to come off shed at Amiens Street, Dublin. The letters CIE on the buffer beam indicate that this was one of the locomotives transferred from the GNRB to CIE in 1958. It was built by North British in 1901, reboilered in 1922 and withdrawn in 1963.

(June 1961). *BLP - C90*

This neat and compact little locomotive is CIE Class J26 0-6-0T 560, still carrying its GSR cast numberplate on the side tank, seen on the turntable at Fenit Pier during an IRRS railtour. It was one of a class of twelve, this engine being built by Kitson in 1893 and withdrawn in 1963. (June 1961). *BLP - C916.*

A picture taken during an IRRS visit to Ennis to see the remnants of the three-foot gauge West Clare Railway during its demolition period. Here railcar 3387, looking very care worn, stands amongst the detritus in the yard. The Railway had closed on 31 January 1961, having become the last survivor of all the Irish narrow gauge railways .No.3387 was one of four railcars built in 1952, the power units, bogies and cabs by Walker Brothers and the coach sections at Inchicore. They were of the well tried type previously built for the CDR. (June 1961). *BLP - C93*

Another locomotive photographed on its home railway is UTA Class U2 4-4-0 74 DUNLUCE CASTLE, seen at Antrim on an IRRS special in June 1961. This engine was built by North British in 1924 to the design of Henry Fowler of the LMS, one of a class of eighteen for the NCC to work all the principal passenger trains on its main line from Belfast to Londonderry. This they did until the advent of the Class W "Moguls" in the next decade. Eleven of the class were named after Castles in Northern Ireland and 74's nameplate is seen attached, but set well back, on the front splasher. Following withdrawal in 1963, 74 was preserved and now resides in the Ulster Folk & Transport Museum at Cultra, resplendent in gleaming LMS/NCC crimson lake livery. Those who bemoan the failure to preserve an LMS 2P 4-4-0 need look no further than this beautiful engine, would that the money were available to restore it to working order!

BLP - C94

Strabane was the point of contact between the three-foot gauge CDR and the five-foot three-inch gauge GNR. This view is looking north at the transfer goods shed with GNR Class U 4-4-0 65 LOUGH MELVIN, by now in the ownership of the UTA, whilst on the left four wheel diesel 11 PHOENIX shunts narrow gauge wagons. PHOENIX was originally built in 1928 by Atkinson-Walker as a steam tractor for the Clogher Valley Railway but was not a success. It was purchased by the County Donegal for 100 guineas (£105) in 1932 and sent to Dundalk for a Gardner 6L2 diesel engine to be fitted. It then spent its life on shunting duties at Strabane, and following closure of the Railway on the last day of 1959 is now preserved at the Ulster Folk & Transport Museum at Cultra.

(August 1959). *BLP - C101*

A view at the west end of Stranorlar, the headquarters of the CDRJC, as 2-6-4T 4 MEENGLAS makes ready to leave with an afternoon goods train to Donegal. The distinctive administrative offices and station are in the background, behind the curving platform which had been used by trains on the Glenties branch until the latter's closure to passengers in 1947 and to goods in 1952.

(August 1959). *BLP - C102*

The last railcar to enter service on the CDR was 20, seen here at Donegal forming a service to Killybegs. The body was built at Dundalk and the engine by Walker Brothers in 1951, the second of two of modern appearance. The Gardner 6LW diesel engine was enclosed within the drivers cab and the passenger section provided 41 seats, with entrances front and rear. In 1961 this railcar and 19 were sold to the Isle of Man Railway where they still remain. The smart lines of this railcar are almost identical to those of the West Clare unit seen at picture C93 on page 45.

(August 1959). *BLP - C103*

Looking north towards the narrow gauge side of Strabane station, there are two of the Donegal 2-6-4T engines shunting. Left is 4 MEENGLAS and right its "younger sister", Class 5a 2 BLANCHE, which came from Nasmyth Wilson in 1912. Fortunately both are preserved, BLANCHE is at the Ulster Folk & Transport Museum at Cultra and MEENGLAS nearer home on the Foyle Valley Railway, Londonderry.

(August 1959). *BLP - C107*

The only example of its class is this unnumbered and nameless Class L2 0-4-2ST seen shunting at Inchicore Wagon Works in June 1961. It was built by the GSWR in 1914 as a service locomotive and named SAMBO, but unnumbered. It remained in use until 1962.

BLP - C111

Between 1959 and 1961 the UTA had two locomotives named LOUGH MELVIN, both acquired from other railways. In 1958 GNR Class U 4-4-0 LOUGH MELVIN came from the GNRB and in 1959 the UTA bought two ex SL & NCR 0-6-4Ts, one of which was LOUGH MELVIN. These two locmotives were built by Beyer Peacock in 1949 and hired to the SL & NCR until closure of that Railway in 1957. The UTA classified the two engines Class Z, and allocated LOUGH MELVIN engine number 26. In very clean condition it is seen outside Adelaide shed, Belfast in August 1959, alongside a Class WT 2-6-4T. 26 was withdrawn in 1968 but its sister engine 27 LOUGH ERNE, is preserved by the RPSI at Whitehead, see picture C42 on page 24.

BLP - C112

One of eight 0-6-0s built by the GSWR in 1903 stands outside Waterford shed on what Keith describes as "an inclement day" in June 1961. It became CIE Class J9 351 and was withdrawn in 1963.

BLP - C113

A rare colour picture of the unique CIE experimental turf burning 0-6-6-0 locomotive CC1. It was designed by Oliver Bulleid, previously Chief Mechanical Engineer of the English Southern Railway, built at Inchicore in 1957 and ran trials in 1957/58, but was never taken into service. It burned milled peat, mechanically fed from bunkers at each end to a central firebox and had a superheater in each smokebox. It had four cylinders, each bogie having two, and the boiler had two barrels. It is seen out of use at Inchicore in June 1961 and was scrapped in 1963.

BLP - C116

CIE Class J15a 0-6-0 703 is seen in steam standing outside Inchicore shed in July 1956. It was one of five locomotives built by the GSWR in 1929 and was withdrawn in 1960.

BLP - C136

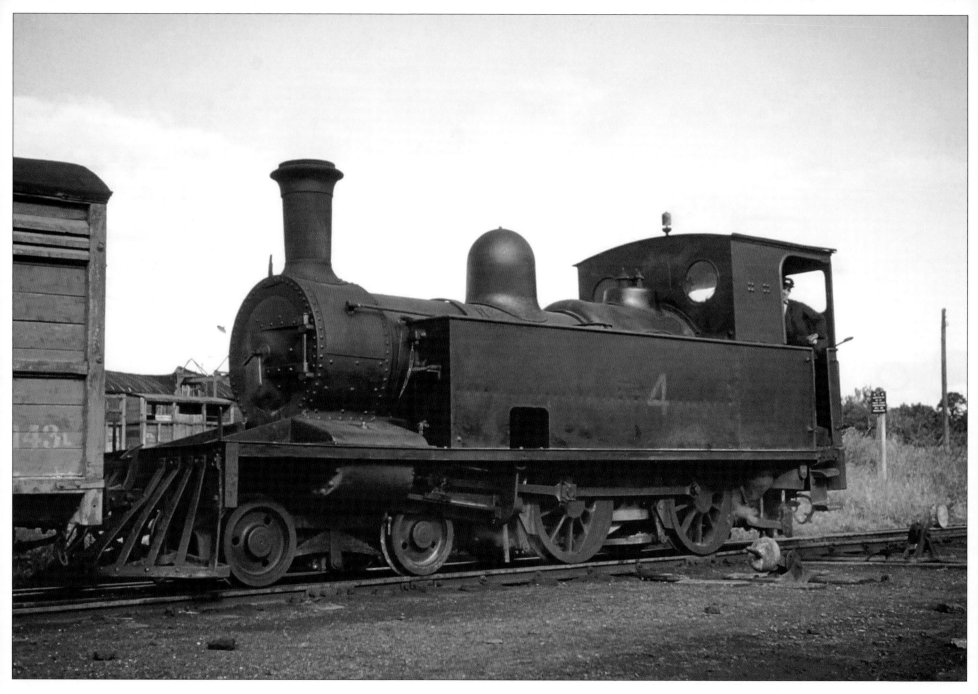

There are not many colour photographs of one of the original C & L narrow gauge 4-4-0Ts and so Keith was fortunate to capture this lovely little engine, 4L, at Dromod in July 1956 looking quite respectable in its all over unrelieved black livery. It was one of eight engines built for the opening of the C & L by Robert Stephensons in 1887 and survived until after the closure of the Railway, being cut up in 1960. Sister engine 2 with its original name KATHLEEN restored, is preserved at the Cultra Museum.　　*BLP - C142*

Standing alongside the water tank at Mohill on the C & L line in July 1956, 4-4-0T 4L is blowing off, having plenty of steam for the remaining five and three quarter miles journey to Dromod with the morning mixed train from Ballinamore.

BLP - C148

The high water mark of GNR express passenger locomotives were the five Class VS 4-4-0s built by Beyer Peacock in 1948 to the design of H.R. McIntosh. They were the last new design of 4-4-0s in the British Isles, and probably in the world, and the only GNR locomotives to have Walschaerts valve gear, smoke deflectors and number plates. All five were named after Irish Rivers. 210 ERNE is seen here at the head of a train at Great Victoria Street station, Belfast in July 1956. Sadly and despite their modernity, no VS was preserved.

BLP - C176

GNR 157 is seen shunting near Adelaide shed in Belfast in July 1956. This was a class QL 4-4-0 built by North British in 1904 and passed to the UTA when the GNRB assets were divided with CIE in 1958, and then withdrawn in the same year.

BLP - C187

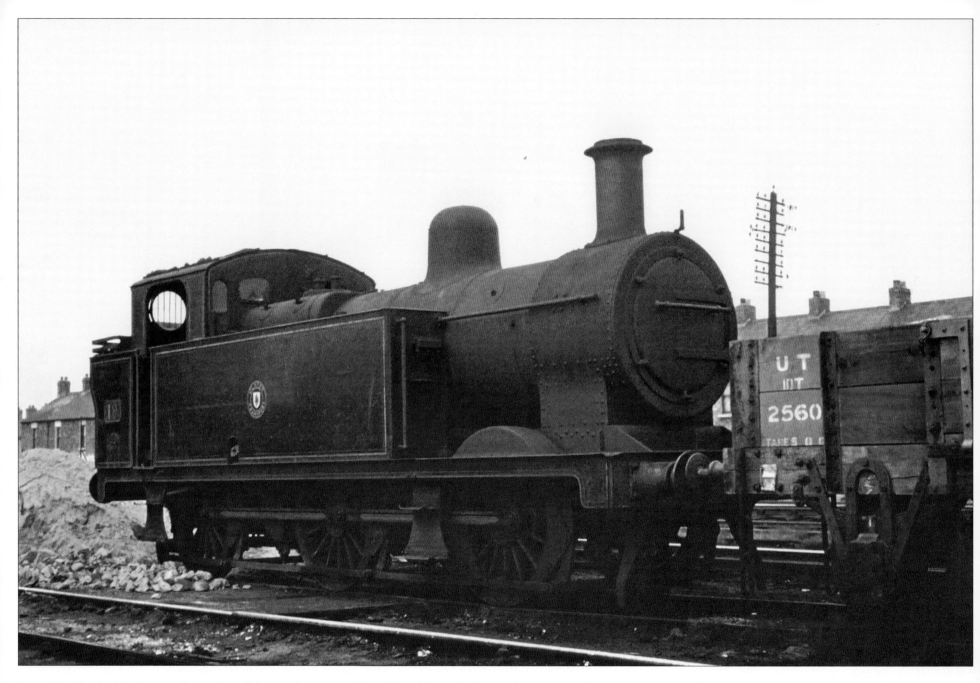

A very familiar looking locomotive to those living on the eastern side of the Irish Sea but in Northern Ireland it was one of a class of just two. To assist with heavy traffic demands during the Second World War, two LMS Class 3F Fowler "Jinty" 0-6-0Ts were regauged (by simply reversing the dished wheel centres on their axle seats and retyring) and sent over to the NCC in 1944. They were the only second hand LMS steam locomotives to work in Ireland. They became class Y and were numbered 18 and 19. This is 19 (ex LMS 7553, built by Hunslet in 1927) by now in UTA livery, shunting at York Road in July 1956. It had outlived its sister (LMS 7456, Bagnall, 1926) by seven years when it was withdrawn in 1963. *BLP - C188*

A portrait of GNR Class SG2 0-6-0 175 standing outside Belfast Adelaide shed, attached to a later style tender. This locomotive was one of a goods class designed by George Glover and built by Beyer Peacock in 1913. (July 1956). *BLP - C190*

61

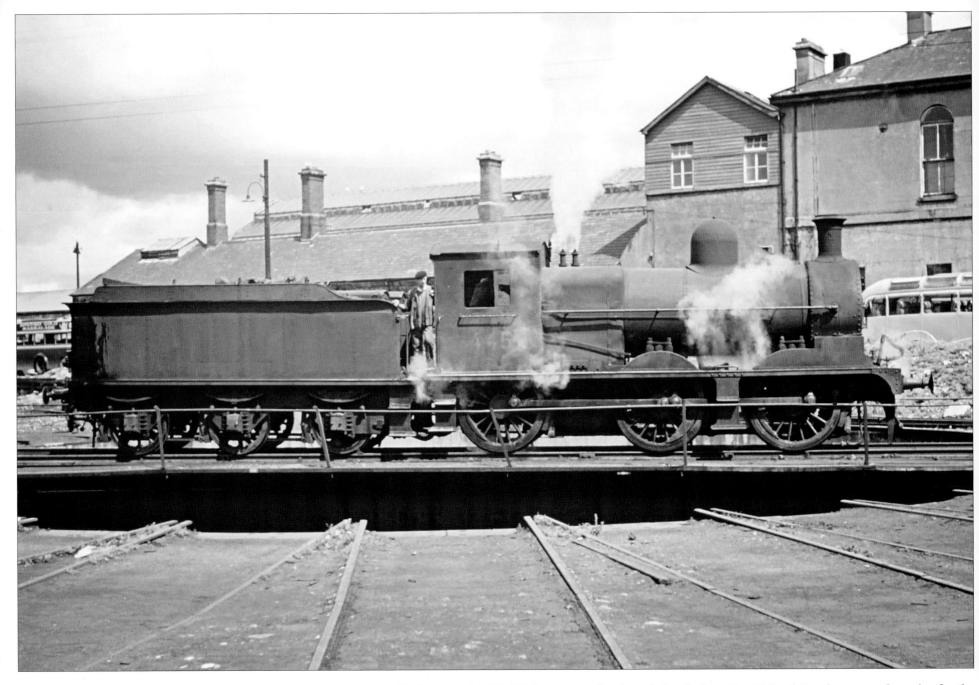

Gently oozing steam as it sits on the turntable at Broadstone shed, Dublin, is Class J8 0-6-0 445. It was one of a class of nine designed by Richard Cronin as a goods engine for the DSER and built by Beyer Peacock in 1905.
(July 1956). *BLP - C192*

A long serving GNR goods engine seen hauling a local passenger train on a sunny evening in July 1956, passing Adelaide and heading south down the main line towards Lisburn. It is Class QG 0-6-0 152, a solid looking locomotive built by North British in 1903, and withdrawn sixty years later from CIE ownership.

BLP - C198

A pair of Atlantic type tank engines gently brewing up outside Adelaide shed, Belfast. Left is Class T2 21 and right Class T1 189. The two classes, designed by George Glover were virtually identical and eventually totalled twenty five locomotives. Numerically they became the largest GNR class, and were mainly but not exclusively, used on suburban trains in the Belfast and Dublin areas. (July 1956). *BLP - C199*

Another locomotive type familiar in outline to those living in Southern England was the SECR Maunsell designed Class N 2-6-0. After the First World War Woolwich Arsenal turned to the manufacture of railway equipment to cushion the rapid rise in unemployment which the cessation of armament production would produce. Following two separate orders from the MGWR in 1923 and the GSR in 1925, at a total knock down price of £58,000 for twenty seven sets of parts, plus four spare boilers, the GSR assembled twenty six locomotives, including 376, seen here at Amiens Street shed in June 1961. This engine was assembled at Broadstone Works in 1926, later under CIE it was classified as a Class K1 and was withdrawn in the year Keith took this picture.

BLP - C202

This small inspection car was built in 1922 for the Tralee & Dingle section but was later transferred to the West Clare Railway. It was originally powered with a Ford Model T engine and transmission and accommodated a driver and three passengers. When it came to the West Clare it was re-engined with a more modern Ford unit. From time to time it visited other GSR/CIE three-foot gauge lines, but following closure of the West Clare on 31 January 1961, it was scrapped at Ennis shortly after this photograph was taken in June 1961.

BLP - C218

Most prestigious of the GNR trains were the express services on the one hundred and twelve miles of main line between Belfast and Dublin. Seen here is Class VS 4-4-0 210 ERNE approaching Amiens Street under a clear signal at the end of its journey from Belfast.
(**July 1956**). *BLP - C233*

Well cleaned for railtour duty is Class J15b 0-6-0 719 seen blowing off at Mullingar station during an IRRS tour in June 1961. The young lad on the platform is admiring the engine and obviously taking a short break from selling confectionery to the passengers from his outsized tray!

BLP - C243

CDR Railcar 10 hauling Trailer 3 (formerly from the Dublin and Blessington Steam Tramway) waits at Strabane station on a service to Donegal in July 1959. On the platform is the Customs Examination point, necessitated because near Clady, en route towards Stranorlar, the Railway crossed the border into the Irish Republic.

BLP - C254

A fine portrait of CDR Railcar 16 at Stranorlar. This was an articulated vehicle built by the GNR/Walker Brothers in 1936. It had a Gardner 6LW 102 hp diesel engine and seated 41 passengers. It provided faithful service until closure of the Railway in December 1959 and was finally scrapped in 1961 after a proposed sale to an American buyer fell through. (July 1959). *BLP - C263*

MEENGLAS is seen crossing the River Mourne Bridge as it starts away from Strabane with a goods train to Stranorlar. This was the largest bridge on the Finn Valley section and had its piers set into the River on screw piles. The GNR line to Omagh is visible on the right. *(July 1959). BLP - C267*

A portrait of Class 5a 2-6-4T 2 BLANCHE taken at Strabane in July 1959. It was one of the three superheated engines supplied by Nasmyth Wilson in 1912 which became the last steam locomotives built for the CDR. BLANCHE is now preserved in the Cultra Museum.

BLP - C268

This vehicle was an interesting acquisition by the County Donegal in 1934 from the scrap merchants who had bought the entire rolling stock of the Dublin & Blessington Steam Tramway after its closure in 1932. It was a Drewry 35 hp petrol engined railcar which could be driven from either end. It was regauged at Stranorlar and became Railcar 3. In 1944 it was rebuilt as a trailer with 40 seats as seen here at Stranorlar in July 1959. It is now preserved in the Ulster Folk & Transport Museum at Cultra. *BLP - C269*

On the CDR, Class 5 2-6-4T 6 COLUMBKILLE's mixed train is being marshalled at Stranorlar for departure to Strabane on a sunny day in July 1956. After closure of the Railway this engine was one of three involved in an abortive sale to an American but fortunately was not scrapped and is now preserved at Londonderry. *BLP - C310*

An everyday event in July 1956, but a sight which still made an attractive picture. The driver of CDR Railcar 15 hands over the staff to the signalman at Stranorlar West Cabin as the train comes into the station from Donegal, complete with two red covered vans in tow.

BLP - C313

The Midland Railway parentage of this goods engine is evident, but the small high pitched boiler and outside framed tender of NCC Class V 0-6-0 14 give it an antiquated appearance which belies its true age. It was one of three designed by Henry Fowler and built at Derby in 1923. It remained in UTA ownership until 1964 and is seen here shunting at York Road, Belfast, in July 1956.

BLP - C314

The GNR Class SG3 0-6-0s were the heaviest 0-6-0 goods engines to work in Ireland. Here is No. 97, built by Beyer Peacock in 1921, and seen at Adelaide shed in July 1956.

BLP - C315

GNR Class T2 4-4-2T 3 is carrying out carriage stock shunting duties at Amiens Street, Dublin. It was built by Beyer Peacock in 1913 and finished its days in CIE stock. (July 1961). *BLP - C320*

An interesting scene at Strabane showing MEENGLAS standing at the County Donegal platform ready to depart with the afternoon goods to Donegal. The substantial covered footbridge spanned the three platforms of the GNR side of the station, on the right, and connected to the narrow gauge island platform. *(August 1959). BLP - C567*

This venerable tank engine, CIE Class F6 2-4-2T 42, is seen shunting coaching stock at Inchicore. It was one of a class of six designed as a passenger class by H A Ivatt when Locomotive Superintendent of the GSWR and built at Inchicore in 1893. Having proved his mettle in Ireland, Ivatt went to England in 1896 to become Locomotive Engineer of the English Great Northern Railway at Doncaster.
(June 1961). *BLP - C912*